SCIENTIST ACADEMY

First American Edition 2017
Kane Miller, A Division of EDC Publishing

Copyright © 2017 Quarto Publishing plc

For information contact:
Kane Miller, A Division of EDC Publishing
PO Box 470663
Tulsa, OK 74147-0663
www.kanemiller.com
www.edcpub.com
www.usbornebooksandmore.com

Library of Congress Control Number: 2016960142
Printed in China

ISBN: 978-1-61067-668-7

2 3 4 5 6 7 8 9 10

SCIENTIST
ACADEMY

WRITTEN BY
STEVE MARTIN

ILLUSTRATED BY
ESSI KIMPIMÄKI

Kane Miller
A DIVISION OF EDC PUBLISHING

CONTENTS

LABORATORY SCIENTIST

INVESTIGATIVE SCIENTIST

SPACE SCIENTIST

EARTH SCIENTIST

LIFE SCIENTIST

SCIENCE FILE

WELCOME TO SCIENTIST ACADEMY!

Congratulations! You have now joined Scientist Academy, where you will learn about a job where you have to know about ... well, EVERYTHING.

Scientists are curious about the world. They are interested in discovering how things work, from the tiniest particles imaginable to the Universe itself ... and, of course, everything in between.

As there is so much to learn, scientists usually specialize. This means they study certain areas of science. For example, a marine biologist is a scientist who learns about life in the ocean, a geologist is a scientist who studies how Earth was made and an astronomer is a scientist who studies the stars and planets.

As you complete the tasks in this book, you will learn about what a scientist needs to be able to do. This includes:

- Asking questions and solving puzzles
- Carrying out experiments
- Collecting evidence and recording data
- Making careful observations.

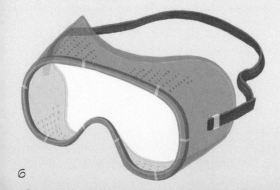

TRAINEE SCIENTIST

FIRST NAME: Avery

LAST NAME: loftus

AGE: 8

DATE JOINED: 7 - 9 - 19

Your first task is to fill in the Trainee Scientist card.

You will also find out about different branches of science and some of the skills and qualities a scientist needs, such as patience, curiosity, a good memory and great teamwork skills.

As you go through the course, you will graduate as a Laboratory Scientist, Investigative Scientist, Space Scientist, Earth Scientist and Life Scientist. Good luck!

MEET THE SCIENTISTS

Before you begin your training, let's meet some of the scientists you will be finding out about at the Academy:

LABORATORY SCIENTISTS

CHEMIST Studies matter (the stuff that makes up everything in the world).

BIOLOGIST Studies everything that is alive. Biologists can specialize in different types of living things.

PHYSICIST Studies how matter moves and is affected by energy and forces.

INVESTIGATIVE SCIENTISTS

CRIME-SCENE SCIENTIST Investigates crime scenes to find evidence and clues.

ARCHEOLOGIST Finds out about the past by studying ancient buildings and objects.

PALEONTOLOGIST Learns about ancient life by studying fossils.

FOOD SCIENTIST Studies what keeps us healthy and creates new foods.

SPACE SCIENTISTS

ASTRONOMER Studies the universe and everything it contains, such as galaxies, stars and planets.

EARTH SCIENTISTS

GEOGRAPHER Studies the features on Earth's surface, such as mountains, rivers and deserts.

GEOLOGIST Studies rocks, volcanoes, earthquakes and how Earth was made.

METEOROLOGIST Observes and explains the weather and climate.

ENVIRONMENTAL SCIENTIST Investigates how the actions of humans affect the natural world.

OCEANOGRAPHER Studies the oceans.

LIFE SCIENTISTS

MARINE BIOLOGIST Learns about the animals and plants that live in the ocean.

ZOOLOGIST Studies the biology and behavior of animals.

SPORTS SCIENTIST Understands the human body and helps athletes improve their performance.

—FAMOUS— SCIENTISTS

All through history, scientists have helped us to learn more about ourselves and the world we live in. Below are six very famous scientists. Read the text to learn about their discoveries and then answer the quiz.

Archimedes (287 BCE—212 BCE)

In ancient Greece, Archimedes discovered that an object under water loses the same weight as the water it replaces—a rule known as the **"Archimedes Principle."** Legend says he noticed this while having a bath, jumped out and ran down the street in the nude, shouting, "Eureka!"

Nicolaus Copernicus (1473—1543)

This famous astronomer was the first to realize that the Sun is at the center of the **Solar System**, with the planets traveling around it. Before this, people thought Earth was at the center.

Isaac Newton (1642—1727)

Sir Isaac Newton helped us to understand the **force of gravity** by explaining how objects pull toward each other. This is why objects fall to Earth. One story says he had this idea when an apple dropped on his head from a tree.

Charles Darwin (1809—1882)

Darwin's study of animals and plants led to his **theory of evolution**, which says that all living things have evolved (changed) over many thousands of years to be better suited to their environment.

Albert Einstein (1879—1955)

The genius, Albert Einstein, is perhaps the most famous scientist of all time. His study of **physics** completely changed the way we understand space, time, light and gravity.

Stephen Hawking (born 1942)

There are still great scientists hard at work. Stephen Hawking has helped us to understand how the Universe began and to learn more about **black holes** (mysterious dark places in space).

TEST YOUR KNOWLEDGE

Read each statement and then circle "True" or "False" in the panel.

1. Archimedes lived more than 2,000 years ago.	**TRUE**	**FALSE**
2. Copernicus found that the Sun is at the center of the Solar System.	**TRUE**	**FALSE**
3. Sir Isaac Newton invented the force of gravity.	**TRUE**	**FALSE**
4. Darwin studied how living things gradually change over time.	**TRUE**	**FALSE**
5. Einstein was one of the most famous chemists of all time.	**TRUE**	**FALSE**
6. Hawking was one of the earliest scientists.	**TRUE**	**FALSE**

When you have finished the quiz, check your answers at the bottom of the page and then place your Task Complete sticker here.

ANSWERS: 1. True. 2. True. 3. False (he discovered gravity but he did not invent it). 4. True. 5. False (he was a physicist). 6. False (he is a modern scientist).

TASK COMPLETE

—PENDULUM—
EXPERIMENT

Begin your science training by carrying out an experiment on a pendulum. This is a hanging weight that swings back and forth when pushed or pulled, like an empty swing.

You need: paper cup, scissors, 63-inch length of string, handful of small pebbles, long stick or broom handle, 2 chairs, tape measure, timer, pencil, adult helper.

1. Ask your adult helper to make a hole in either side of the paper cup. Poke the string ends through the two holes and tie them together. Put 3 or 4 pebbles inside the cup.

2. Place the chairs back-to-back. Loop the string and cup over the stick and balance the stick across the chairs.

3. With the pendulum hanging centrally, measure from the top of the string to the cup (about 31.5 inches). Write the measurement in the space (Test One) on the opposite page.

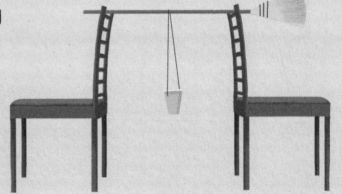

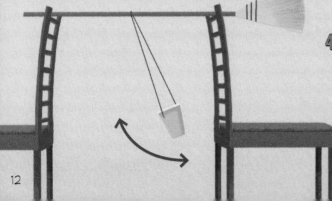

4. Gently pull the cup back and up and then let go. Count how many swings the pendulum makes in one minute (use the timer) and write down your answer. Repeat the experiment, following the instructions for Tests Two and Three.

TEST ONE

LENGTH OF STRING

NUMBER OF SWINGS

TEST TWO

Repeat the experiment, but this time **double the weight** inside the cup.

LENGTH OF STRING

NUMBER OF SWINGS

TEST THREE

Repeat the experiment with the first weight, but this time **shorten the string** by half.

LENGTH OF STRING

NUMBER OF SWINGS

CONCLUSION

What you find out from your experiment is called the conclusion. Write yours in the spaces below.

What happens when you use a heavier weight? _____

_____

_____

What happens when you shorten the string? _____

_____

_____

PLACE STICKER HERE

When you have finished the experiment and recorded the results, place your Task Complete sticker here.

TASK COMPLETE

13

IN THE LABORATORY

Scientists often work in a specially equipped room called a laboratory. This is where all the scientific tools and equipment they need to carry out tests, observations and experiments are kept. Here is some of the equipment scientists keep in their laboratory.

LAB COAT

SCALES are used to carefully **weigh** items.

SAFETY is very important in the laboratory. Scientists handling chemicals wear **protective** clothing to keep them from harm.

GLOVES

GOGGLES

A **THERMOMETER** is used to measure **temperature**.

TEST TUBES are small, clear containers used to store, mix and **experiment** with liquids.

A **BEAKER** is **larger** than a test tube, but is used for a similar purpose.

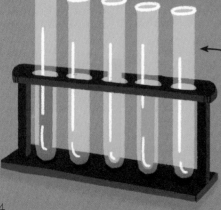

HOME LAB EXPERIMENT

You are going to carry out your own laboratory experiment. Don't worry if you don't have a fully equipped laboratory at home. The only scientific item you need is a beaker, or you can use a clear plastic or clean glass jar instead.

You need: beaker (empty plastic or glass jar), water, vegetable oil, one or more food colorings, adult observer.

1. Half fill the beaker with cold water.

Water

Oil

2. Slowly pour the vegetable oil on top of the water until it is about 1.5 to 2 inches thick. Notice that the oil and water do not mix!

3. Add about 8 drops of food coloring. These drops can all be the same color or different colors. The drops will stay as drops, before sinking to the bottom of the oil and then mixing with the water.

WHAT JUST HAPPENED?

One of the reasons oil and water don't mix is because water **molecules** (the smallest particles) are packed together more tightly than oil molecules. This is something scientists call **"density."** Because the oil's density is less, it floats on top of the water. The food coloring has a similar density to water, so mixes with it easily.

When you have finished the home lab experiment, place your Task Complete sticker here.

TASK COMPLETE

MEASURING SKILLS

A trainee scientist needs to learn lots of different skills, and measuring is one of the most important. Laboratory scientists have to be able to measure lengths, temperature, amounts and time accurately.

Try the tasks on these pages for practice.

1 You have to heat a liquid gently for 45 minutes. The start time is shown below. Which is the correct finish time? Circle your answer.

START TIME

| 2:45 | 3:15 | 3:30 |

2 The two thermometers show the temperature in degrees Fahrenheit at the start and end of an experiment. By how much has the temperature increased? Put your answer in the box.

START

50 60 70 80 90 100 110 120 130 140

END

50 60 70 80 90 100 110 120 130 140

70

3 How much does this box weigh? Circle your answer.

A. 4 lb.

B. 4.5 lb.

C. 5.4 lb.

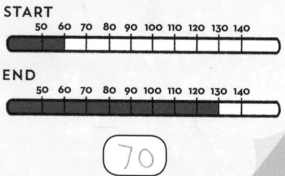

COMPARE THE PAIRS

These measuring tasks are slightly different. Look at each pair and decide which line is longer—A or B. Write down your answers and then measure the lines again using a ruler. The results might surprise you!

PAIR ONE

Which horizontal line (the lines going straight across) is longer?

BEFORE MEASURING   *A*

AFTER MEASURING   *same*

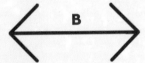

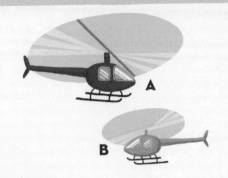

PAIR TWO

Which helicopter rotor blade is longer?

BEFORE MEASURING   *A*

AFTER MEASURING   *same*

PAIR THREE

Which blue line is longer?

BEFORE MEASURING   *B*

AFTER MEASURING   *same*

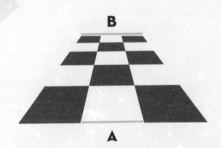

When you have finished the measuring tasks, check your answers at the bottom of the page and then place your Task Complete sticker here.

ANSWERS: 1. Time = 3:15. 2. Temperature = 70 degrees. 3. Weight = 4.5 lb.
Each pair of lines in pairs 1, 2 and 3 are the same length.

TASK COMPLETE

17

THE CHEMIST

A chemist is a scientist who studies chemicals—the matter (all solids, liquids and gases) that makes up everything in the world around us. Chemists carry out experiments to find out about the different chemicals. They explore what they are made of and how they interact with each other.

A trainee scientist needs to understand **scientific language**. Here are some important words used by chemists and what they mean.

CHEMICAL ELEMENT A chemical element cannot be **broken down** into anything smaller. Two different elements —hydrogen (H) and oxygen (O)—are the chemical ingredients of water.

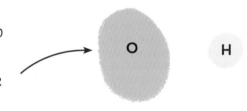

CHEMICAL COMPOUND When two or more chemical elements **join together**, this forms a new type of matter called a compound. So, water (or H_2O) is a chemical compound.

CHEMICAL REACTION When two or more chemicals **react** together to form a new substance, a chemical reaction has taken place. For example, when vinegar (acetic acid) is added to baking soda, carbon dioxide gas is formed.

GAS BUBBLES

VINEGAR

BAKING SODA

INVISIBLE INK
Create a chemical reaction and learn how to make invisible ink.

You need: half a lemon, cup, sheet of white paper, paintbrush or cotton swab, light bulb, adult helper.

1. Squeeze the lemon juice into the cup.

2. Dip the paintbrush or cotton swab into the juice and then write or draw a secret message on the paper. You will have to keep dipping into the juice as you go.

3. Wait for the juice to dry and become invisible.

4. To reveal the message, you need to heat the ink. Ask your adult helper to switch on the light bulb, and help you hold the paper close to it. Now watch your message appear.

EUREKA!
The heat from the lamp causes a **chemical reaction** between the paper and the lemon juice, causing it to turn brown.

When you have finished the chemical reaction experiment, place your Task Complete sticker here.

PLACE STICKER HERE

TASK COMPLETE

THE
BIOLOGIST

Biologists investigate what plants, animals and human beings are made from, and how they stay alive. Here, you can learn about the major organs that keep your body working.

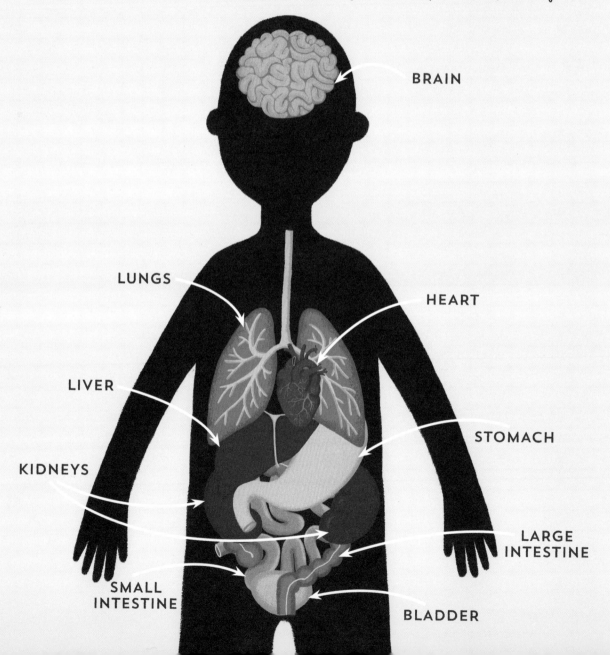

BRAIN

LUNGS

HEART

LIVER

STOMACH

KIDNEYS

LARGE
INTESTINE

SMALL
INTESTINE

BLADDER

BRAIN The brain controls all the **tasks** your body needs to carry out, like breathing and the beating of your heart. It is also the organ you use for thinking, learning and remembering.

HEART The heart **pumps** blood around your body, supplying it with oxygen and nutrients (food).

LUNGS You use your lungs every time you **breathe**. They take in oxygen from the air and send it to the blood. They then take a waste gas called carbon dioxide from the blood and you breathe it out.

LIVER The liver has several jobs. It makes and sends something called bile to the stomach to digest food. It **stores** sugar and releases it when the body needs it, and it gets rid of harmful substances in the blood.

STOMACH Your stomach **releases** chemicals that start digesting the food you have swallowed.

SMALL INTESTINE Pieces of food are pushed from the stomach into this tube, to be **digested** (broken down) and taken in by the body. In an average adult, this tube is around 16.5 feet long!

LARGE INTESTINE The large intestine is about 5 feet long. It helps to digest food and receives the undigested food and **waste** the body gets rid of when you go to the bathroom.

KIDNEYS The kidneys **clean** your blood, filtering out waste and harmful substances. These are sent to the bladder.

BLADDER The waste **liquid** from the kidneys is stored here. It leaves the body when you go to the bathroom.

THE PHYSICIST

Physicists are scientists who study the physical world. The things that you can touch and feel are all made up of matter, and this is what physicists are interested in. They look at how matter behaves, and examine the energy and forces that affect it.

FLOATING PING-PONG BALL EXPERIMENT

Investigate what happens when two forces act on an object. You will use one force to push the object upward and balance this with gravity—the force that pulls objects toward each other.

You need: hair dryer, ping-pong ball, adult helper.

AIRFLOW

GRAVITY

1. Ask the adult to switch on the hair dryer to its highest setting.

2. Point the dryer straight up, carefully place the ping-pong ball into the airflow and watch it shoot upward.

3. The ball will move up until the pushing force of the airflow is balanced by the pulling force of gravity. When the ball reaches this point, it will float!

When you have finished the floating ball experiment, place your Task Complete sticker here.

GRAVITY IS THE FORCE THAT PULLS OBJECTS TOWARD EACH OTHER. EARTH PULLS APPLES TO THE GROUND.

TASK COMPLETE

Congratulations! You are now a...

LABORATORY SCIENTIST
— GRADUATE —

NAME: ------------------------------------

The above-named trainee
has now completed the

LABORATORY SCIENTIST
course.

Scientist Academy would like
to wish you every success
in your career.

GOOD LUCK!

DATE: ------------------------------------

INVESTIGATIVE SCIENTIST

BRAIN TRAINING

Scientists have to spend a lot of their time working things out because much of their job involves solving puzzles. These logical-thinking challenges will help you to think like a scientist!

SCIENCE SQUARE

Fill in the blank squares to complete the grid. Each row (line across) and each column (line down) must have only one of each item. There are four to choose from:

Test tube

Magnifying glass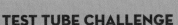

Magnet

Light bulb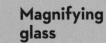

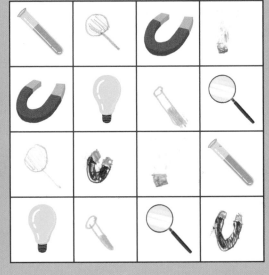

TEST TUBE CHALLENGE

Identify the correct liquid from the row of test tubes. Use the clues below to help you, crossing out the test tubes that don't fit as you go.

- It is a blue liquid.
- It isn't next to a red test tube.
- The test tube is over half full.
- The test tube has a stopper.

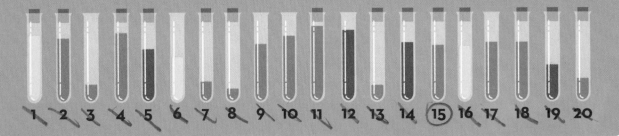

PLOT THE PATHS

Draw lines to join beakers that are the same color. None of your lines can cross! We have done the first one for you. The answer is on page 64.

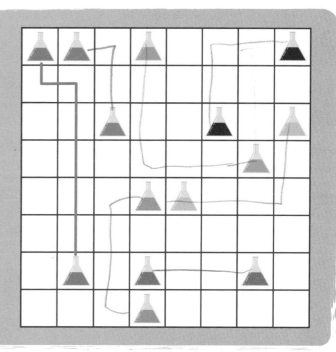

HOW MANY TRIANGLES AND SQUARES?

To help you find all of the triangles and squares in this shape, trace over it three times and then color and number each smaller shape.

You need: tracing or thin paper, pencils, crayons or pens.

Write your answers here:

Squares **2**   Triangles **10**

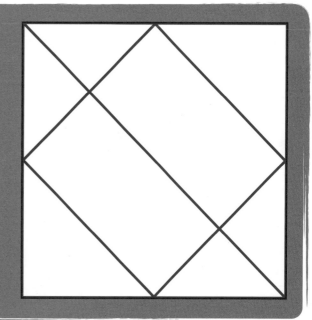

When you have finished the logical-thinking challenges, check your answers at the bottom of the page and then place your sticker here.

TASK COMPLETE

25

CRIME-SCENE — SCIENCE —

There are all sorts of scientists who specialize in different types of work. A crime-scene specialist uses their scientific knowledge to help the police track down criminals. Like all scientists, a crime-scene scientist must have excellent observation skills.

To get a good idea of the **work** a crime-scene scientist does, you are going to complete three tasks. They will help the police **track down** the leader of a gang of bank robbers!

TRACKS MATCH

Your first task is to identify which gang carried out the theft. Luckily, the getaway car left tire tracks at the scene. Match the tracks to the right car to see which gang was involved.

TRACKS AT THE
CRIME SCENE

THE BADDY BANDITS

THE CRAFTY CROOKS

THE ROWDY ROBBERS

THE TRICKY THIEVES

When you've matched the tracks, check your answer at the bottom of the page and then tackle the next task!

ANSWER: The tire tracks were left by the Rowdy Robbers.

FINGERPRINT ID

It's time to use your scientific thinking skills. The witness said the leader came through the door first, so you need to check it for fingerprints. Look carefully—which two robbers left their fingerprints on the door? Circle your answers.

FINGERPRINTS ON DOOR

WICKED WALTER	CROOKED KEVIN	BAD BRAD	GARY THE GANGSTER	SHADY STEVE

HANDWRITING TEST

Okay! You've narrowed it down to two suspects. The gang leader handed the witness a note with the words, "It's a robbery!" written on it, so get your suspects to write down exactly the same words. Now compare their handwriting to the note to see which suspect wrote it and circle your answer.

IT'S A ROBBERY!

THE ROBBERY NOTE

IT'S A ROBBERY!

BAD BRAD

IT'S A ROBBERY!

SHADY STEVE

When you've identified the gang leader, check your answer at the bottom of the page and then place your sticker here.

TASK COMPLETE

HISTORY DETECTIVE

Archeologists are both scientists and historians. They use their scientific skills to examine ancient buildings and objects to find out about our history. First though, they have to find the historic remains.

The remains are often buried underground, but the archeologist can use a scientific instrument called a **radar scanner** to find them. As the archeologist wheels the radar scanner across an area, it sends energy waves into the ground. The scanner records the returning wave signals. They can show the archeologist how far down to dig—and even what to dig for.

A **transmitter** sends energy waves into the ground. A **receiver** picks up the returning waves.

When the energy waves hit a buried object, they **bounce** back to the scanner.

ENERGY WAVES EXPERIMENT

To help you understand how moving energy waves can bounce back to a receiver, you are going to make a musical instrument and use it to experiment with sound waves.

You need: empty tissue box, long elastic bands.

1. Take off any clear plastic covering the hole in the top of the tissue box. Stretch the elastic bands around the box and over the hole.

2. Now twang the bands to send sound waves bouncing up from inside the box toward a receiver — your ear.

RECEIVER

TRANSMITTER

You can experiment with the way the sound waves travel. Remove the elastic bands, stuff the box with a T-shirt, replace the bands and twang them. The sound is much quieter because the T-shirt is stopping the path of the sound waves.

When you have finished the energy waves experiment, place your sticker here.

PLACE STICKER HERE

TASK COMPLETE

—FOSSIL— SCIENCE

A paleontologist is another type of scientist who investigates life in the past. They study fossils to learn about life millions of years ago. Fossils are the shapes preserved inside rocks by animal or plant remains. A trainee paleontologist needs to understand how fossils form.

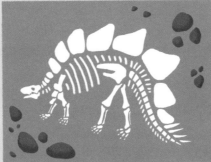

1. A dinosaur died and its body rested on a **riverbed**. Mud or sand gradually buried the skeleton.

2. Over many millions of years, the mud or sand turned to **stone**.

3. The skeleton rotted away but left a **hollow** space in the stone. This space was in the same shape as the skeleton.

4. The space slowly filled with minerals—tiny substances seeping out of nearby rocks —that **hardened**. It is as if the minerals formed a statue of the skeleton.

BRING A FOSSIL TO LIFE

Part of a paleontologist's job is to work out what an extinct creature might have looked like when it was alive. Study the fossil on the opposite page and then draw and color in your idea of this prehistoric dinosaur.

When you have finished the drawing of your imaginary dinosaur, place your Task Complete sticker here.

TASK COMPLETE

FOOD SCIENCE

Food scientists make sure that our food is safe to eat and carry out research to see how healthy it is. They also invent new, tasty foods. This list shows you some of the most important tasks that make up a food scientist's job:

- Finding ways to keep food **fresh** and good to eat for as long as possible.

- Providing **information** on food that is then printed on labels. (Look at some of the cans and boxes in your home to see the kind of information that is given.)

- Discovering **new** ways to produce food efficiently and cheaply.

- **Testing** food and drink to make sure they are safe.

- Inventing foods by creating new **flavors** and products.

- Researching ways to make food products **healthier**, for example, by reducing the amount of sugar or salt.

- Carrying out quality **checks** in food-producing factories, to make sure the food is good enough to be sold in stores.

SCIENTIST INFO

Congratulations! You are now an...

INVESTIGATIVE SCIENTIST
— GRADUATE —

NAME: _____

The above-named trainee
has now completed the

INVESTIGATIVE SCIENTIST

course.

Scientist Academy would like
to wish you every success
in your career.

GOOD LUCK!

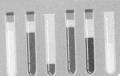

DATE: _____

SKY WATCH

Astronomers are space scientists who study the Universe. They can't bring the Universe into a laboratory, so they spend a lot of time watching the skies and observing the stars and planets.

COMET

SPIRAL GALAXY

ASTEROIDS

PLANET

SATELLITE

INTERNATIONAL SPACE STATION

METEOR SHOWER

DWARF STAR

LITTLE DIPPER CONSTELLATION

BIG DIPPER CONSTELLATION

SPOT THE DIFFERENCES

An astronomer must have excellent observation skills. Practice yours by studying the two night skies on these pages, and circling the eight differences in the night sky below compared to the one on the left.

When you have spotted all eight differences, check the answers at the bottom of the page and then place your Task Complete sticker in the space below.

TASK COMPLETE

INVESTIGATE AN ECLIPSE

Our nearest neighbor, the Moon, is a good place for the trainee scientist to start finding out about space. The Moon can cause a very strange effect here on Earth, called a solar eclipse, which can make day seem like night.

A solar eclipse happens if the Moon lines up with Earth and the Sun during its orbit (journey) around Earth. This blocks the Sun's rays.

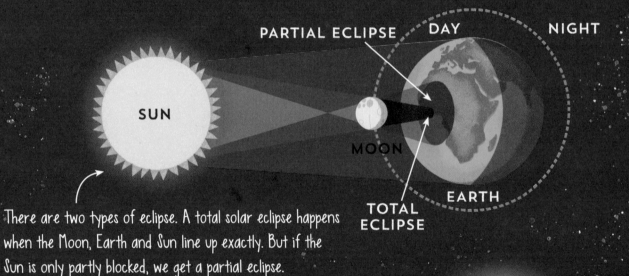

There are two types of eclipse. A total solar eclipse happens when the Moon, Earth and Sun line up exactly. But if the Sun is only partly blocked, we get a partial eclipse.

On Earth, when the Moon covers part of the Sun, you see a partial solar eclipse.

This is the view from Earth during a total solar eclipse: the Moon covers the Sun and blocks out its light, making it go completely dark!

MAKE A MODEL ECLIPSE

It is a scientist's job to explain how and why things happen. Set up a model of a solar eclipse to see how a real one works!

You need: flashlight, small ball, large ball, two friends, a dark room.

1. Get one friend to shine the flashlight (this is the Sun).

2. Get the other friend to stand about 2 feet away from the flashlight and hold up the small ball (the Moon).

3. Hold the large ball about 6 inches from the small ball. Two types of shadow should appear on the large ball—the dark shadow of a total eclipse, surrounded by the lighter shadow of a partial eclipse.

6 in.

24 in.

What happens if you move the flashlight or change the distance between the objects? Try it!

When you have created the solar eclipse model, place your Task Complete sticker here.

TASK COMPLETE

37

SPACE
—TIME—

There are eight planets orbiting (circling around) the Sun in the Solar System. Every time a planet completes one orbit, that makes one year on that planet. The farther away a planet is from the Sun, the longer its orbit. This means that each planet's year is a different length.

JUPITER = 11 YEARS 315 DAYS

URANUS = 84 YEARS

SATURN = 29 YEARS 167 DAYS

VENUS = 225 DAYS

MERCURY = 88 DAYS

EARTH = 365 DAYS

NEPTUNE = 164 YEARS 281 DAYS

MARS = 1 YEAR 321 DAYS

Read the labels to find out
how much Earth-time equals one year
on each planet in the Solar System.

CALCULATE YOUR SPACE AGE

Scientists use a lot of numbers in their work. Practice your math skills by working out how old you would be if you were born on another planet.

You won't be using the exact figures to work out your approximate age on these four planets, but they will be close enough. Write your answers in the boxes.

YOU MIGHT NEED A CALCULATOR TO HELP YOU.

MERCURY
Multiply your Earth age by 4 to see how old you would be on Mercury.

 40

VENUS
Halve your Earth age, then multiply the answer by 3 to find out how old you would be on Venus.

 30

MARS
Halve your Earth age to calculate your approximate age on Mars.

 0

JUPITER
Divide your age by 12 to find out how old you are on Jupiter. You will either be zero or one. So, if you were born on Jupiter, you'd be a baby.

 0

MAKE A SUNDIAL

You can use the rotation of Earth around the Sun to tell the time using a simple device called a sundial. You'll find a press-out model on the cover flaps of this book. The lines show the hours of the day. You will need a compass. On a sunny day, place the sundial outside so that the arrow faces North if you are in the Northern Hemisphere and South if you are in the Southern Hemisphere. As the hours pass, the shadow cast by the sun will move across the dial allowing you to tell the time.

SATELLITES

Artificial satellites are objects that are sent into space to orbit Earth and to carry out various tasks. There are thousands of satellites traveling around our planet. The work they do can be split into three main types:

COMMUNICATION SATELLITES

send information around the world. The information travels as **signals** from phones, TVs, the Internet and other sources. As Earth is round and most signals move in **straight lines**, they are sent up to satellites, which then bounce them back to Earth.

SURVEY SATELLITES

take **photographs** and gather information. Some point toward **Earth** and take pictures of our planet, and some point out into **space** where they have much clearer views than any telescope on Earth.

NAVIGATION SATELLITES allow us to find our way around.
Information from different navigation satellites is used to plot our **position** and the location of places or objects anywhere in the world.

SEE HOW SATELLITE SIGNALS TRAVEL

This challenge shows how a communication satellite helps information traveling in a straight line to "bounce" around an obstacle, such as Earth.

You need: plastic bucket, obstacle (such as a sweater), tennis ball, wall.

1. Place the bucket about 6.5 feet from a wall. It should be on its side, with the open end facing the wall.

2. Keeping level with the bucket and facing the wall, move about 10 feet sideways. Place your obstacle between you and the bucket.

3. Grab the tennis ball and check that you are standing around 6.5 feet away from the wall. Now bounce the ball off the wall so that it goes into the bucket!

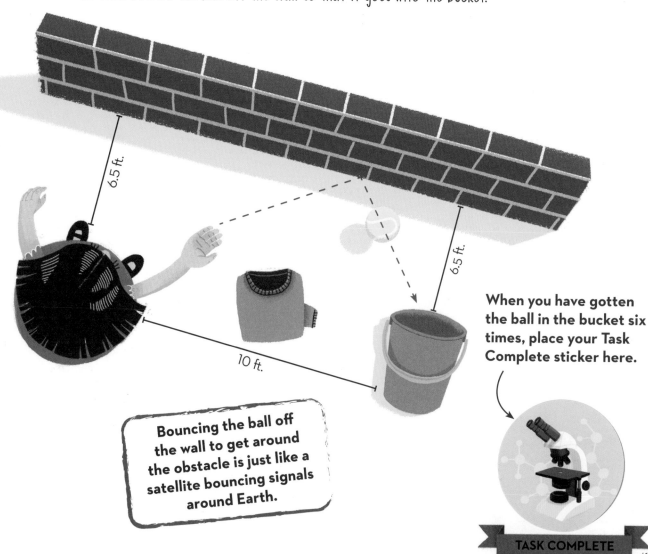

6.5 ft.

6.5 ft.

10 ft.

When you have gotten the ball in the bucket six times, place your Task Complete sticker here.

Bouncing the ball off the wall to get around the obstacle is just like a satellite bouncing signals around Earth.

TASK COMPLETE

41

HOW BIG IS THE —UNIVERSE?—

The Sun is a star at the center of the Solar System, with Earth and seven more planets spinning around it. Farther out in the Solar System lies the dwarf planet Pluto—it is an amazing 3.6 BILLION miles from the Sun! It's very hard to imagine just how far this is.

SUN

MERCURY

VENUS

EARTH

MARS

JUPITER

SATURN

URANUS

NEPTUNE

PLUTO

A car moving at 70 mph, 24 hours a day, 365 days a year, would take over **5,700 years** to travel from the Sun to Pluto!

THE MILKY WAY

Our Solar System is part of a **galaxy** (a group of stars) called the Milky Way. It contains about—wait for it—**100 billion** stars!

OUR
SOLAR
SYSTEM

And there are at least 100 billion galaxies in the Universe! Think of it this way—if the **Universe** was the same size as **Earth**, not only our planet, but the entire **Solar System** would be too tiny to see!

Congratulations! You are now a...

SPACE SCIENTIST
— GRADUATE —

NAME: -

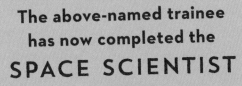

The above-named trainee
has now completed the

SPACE SCIENTIST
course.

Scientist Academy would like
to wish you every success
in your career.

GOOD LUCK!

DATE: -

EARTH SCIENTIST

MAKE A MAP

Geographers study Earth's natural features, such as mountains, rivers, forests and deserts. They understand how the features formed and will change over time, and how people can change the land. Like all scientists, geographers need good observation skills. Practice yours by making a map of the picture below.

Study where the mountains, town, river, lake, railroad line, roads, forests, wind turbines and historic ruin are in the picture. Then copy and place the symbols onto your map.

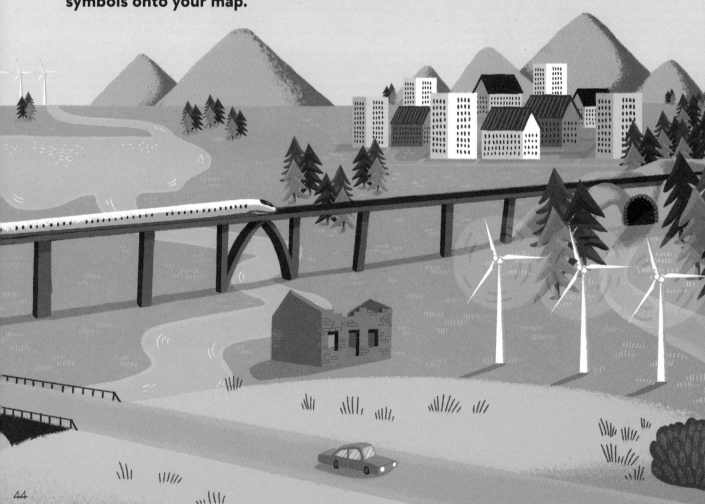

MAP SYMBOLS KEY

 FOREST

 LAKE

 RIVER

WIND TURBINE

 TOWN

 RAILROAD

 MOUNTAIN

ROAD

HISTORIC RUIN

TASK COMPLETE

When you have finished the map, place your Task Complete sticker here.

Draw your map here. The first symbol, the lake, has already been added.

SCIENCE ROCKS!

Geologists study how our planet is made and what happens when powerful natural forces affect it. One important job they do is to monitor the size and strength of earthquakes. A machine called a seismograph records the seismic waves (vibrations) of the shaking ground.

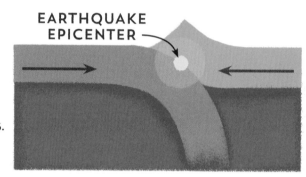

EARTHQUAKE EPICENTER

Earth's surface is made up of huge blocks of rock called **tectonic plates**.

When two plates **push** past each other, the pressure can cause an earthquake.

MAKE AND TEST A SEISMOGRAPH

You need: cardboard box, scissors, paper cup, string, pencil, modeling clay, paper sheet, friend, adult helper.

1. Place the box with the open side facing you. Get your adult helper to use the tip of the scissors to punch two small holes in the top, and to cut an 8-inch-long slot in the back.

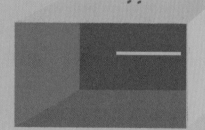

2. Ask your helper to punch two holes—one on either side—near the top of the cup and a third hole through the base. Thread the string through the top holes and push your pencil halfway through the hole in the base.

3. Put enough modeling clay in the cup to weigh it down and to keep the pencil steady. Thread the loose string ends through the holes in the top of the box. Make sure the pencil tip rests on the box base. Knot the loose strings together.

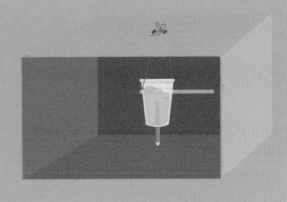

4. Cut a strip of paper about 6 inches wide. Feed it through the slot at the back of the box so the pencil rests on it.

5. Put the box on a table. Ask your friend to shake the box while you pull the paper through and watch the pencil record the seismic waves!

When you have made and tested the seismograph, place your Task Complete sticker here.

PLACE STICKER HERE

TASK COMPLETE

WEATHER WATCHERS

Scientists who study the weather are called meteorologists. They do this so they can predict what conditions are going to be like in the next few days (a short-range weather forecast) and over a longer period (a long-range weather forecast).

DATA

Meteorologists collect data (information) from **weather stations** on land and **satellites** in space about conditions such as air temperature and pressure, wind speeds and the amount of humidity (moisture) in the air.

They use special equipment to record the data:

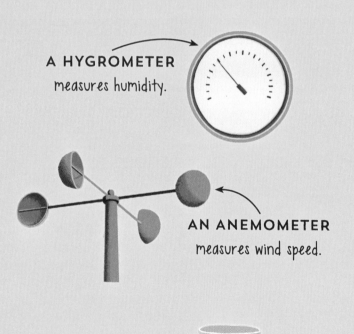

A HYGROMETER
measures humidity.

AN ANEMOMETER
measures wind speed.

A RAIN GAUGE
measures rainfall.

An accurate **weather forecast** can be a real lifesaver for ships' crews and aircraft pilots. Knowing if a bad storm is coming means they can plan ahead and stay safe.

MAKE A WEATHER VANE

A weather vane tells you the direction the wind is blowing from.

You need: Thin cardboard, scissors, drinking straw, tape, paper plate, paper cup, markers, pencil with an eraser on the top, ruler, pin, compass, pebbles, adult helper.

1. Cut a square of cardboard about 3.5 x 3.5 inches. (You can use a cereal box.)

2. Cut an arrowhead triangle shape, measuring about 2.4 inches from base to tip.

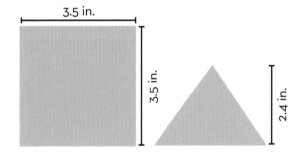

3. Ask an adult helper to snip a slit in each end of the straw. Slide in the paper pieces and tape them in place.

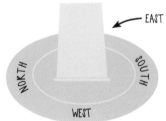

4. Glue the cup upside down on the plate. Write "North," "East," "South" and "West" around the plate in the places shown.

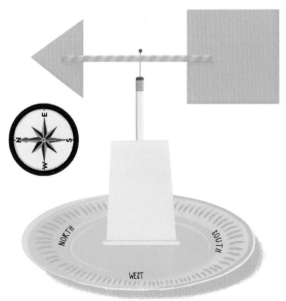

5. Carefully push the pencil through the top of the cup. Mark the center of the straw and get your adult helper to push the pin through it, into the top of the pencil.

6. Place the weather vane outside in a place where it will catch the wind. Use the compass to line up "North" on the plate with north on the compass. Weigh the plate down with pebbles.

When you have made and tested the weather vane, place your Task Complete sticker here.

PLACE STICKER HERE

When the wind blows, the arrow will point to the direction the wind is coming from!

TASK COMPLETE

49

PROTECTING THE PLANET

Environmental scientists study the relationship between Earth and living things. They use this knowledge to work out ways of protecting the natural world from harm, so that plants, animals and people are able to stay healthy.

RAIN FOREST RESCUE

For example, environmental scientists are looking at ways **humans** can protect the huge **Amazon Rain Forest.** The millions upon millions of trees in the forest do an important job: they take carbon dioxide out of the air and release the oxygen we need to breathe.

THE AMAZON RAIN FOREST IN SOUTH AMERICA IS HOME TO ONE IN EVERY 10 OF EARTH'S ANIMAL SPECIES.

NORTH AMERICA

Our planet is home to millions of types of **animals** and **plants.** Each kind lives in the environment (surroundings) that suits its own needs.

PACIFIC OCEAN

ATLANTIC OCEAN

SOUTH AMERICA

RAIN FOREST I-SPY

Part of an environmental scientist's job is to study animals in their natural surroundings. Many rain forest insects use camouflage to help them stay hidden. A leaf katydid looks like a leaf with legs! See if you can find the eight katydids in this picture.

When you have found all eight leaf katydids, place your Task Complete sticker here.

TASK COMPLETE

OCEAN SCIENCE

Oceanographers are scientists who study the world's oceans—and there's a lot to discover. Take a look at these awesome facts and figures.

71% of Earth's surface is covered by seas and oceans. That means over **twice as much** of our planet is covered by ocean than by land.

50%–85% of the **oxygen** we breathe is made by phytoplankton (tiny plants) that live in the oceans.

1,000 YEARS is how long it can take water to make its around-the-world **trip** on the oceans' flowing currents.

97% of the world's water is in the **oceans**. 2% is trapped in **ice** and only 1% is **freshwater**.

36,069 FEET is the depth of the **Mariana Trench**—it is the deepest point in the oceans!

80% of volcanic eruptions and most of the world's **earthquakes** take place under the ocean.

49,709 MILES is the length of the underwater **Mid-Oceanic Ridge**, the world's longest mountain range.

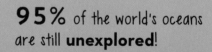

95% of the world's oceans are still **unexplored**!

Congratulations! You are now an...

EARTH SCIENTIST
— GRADUATE —

NAME: _

The above-named trainee
has now completed the
EARTH SCIENTIST
course.

Scientist Academy would like
to wish you every success
in your career.

GOOD LUCK!

DATE: _

FOOD CHAIN

Marine biologists study animals and plants living in the oceans. Many fish, octopuses, sponges and other sea creatures live among coral reefs, which are made from the skeletons of a creature called coral. The creatures in a reef depend upon each other for survival, with one providing food for another as part of a food chain.

In the **Great Barrier Reef**, off the coast of Australia, marine algae are eaten by shrimps, which are eaten by box jellyfish, which are eaten by sea turtles, which are eaten by tiger sharks.

WHO EATS WHOM?

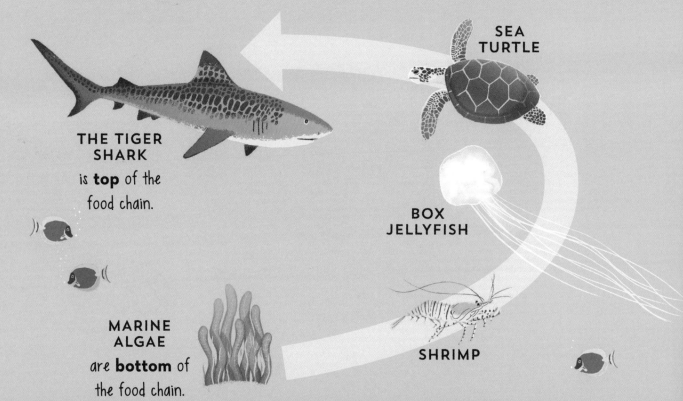

SEA TURTLE

THE TIGER SHARK is **top** of the food chain.

BOX JELLYFISH

MARINE ALGAE are **bottom** of the food chain.

SHRIMP

CORAL REEF MAZE
Link the hunters to their food sources without crossing over any coral!

When you have connected the food chain, place your Task Complete sticker here.

TASK COMPLETE

ANIMAL ID

Zoologists study everything about animals. They learn how their bodies work, how they behave and about the environments they live in. A zoologist needs excellent observation skills! Practice yours by matching the stickers at the back of the book to the animal outlines here.

STORK The stork's long legs help it to **wade** through water looking for food. It catches small animals and fish in its long bill.

IMPALA This is a type of antelope with reddish fur. Impala gather in large herds and graze on grass and shrubs. The males have long **spiral** horns.

AARDVARK This animal uses its long nose and **sticky tongue** to find and catch insects. It avoids the hot sun by sleeping during the day.

MONGOOSE These fur-covered creatures live in **burrows**. They have long bodies and short snouts and ears.

JACKAL Jackals are members of the dog family and live in packs. They are **nocturnal**, sleeping during the day and being active at night.

VULTURE This scavenger feeds on dead animals. It has strong eyesight and a wide **wingspan**, and it can soar for long periods searching for prey.

AFRICAN BUFFALO This powerful, **horned** animal can weigh as much as one ton!

BUSH BABY This nocturnal animal is a **primate**. It got its name because it makes a noise like a screaming baby.

PORCUPINE This rodent is around 23 inches long and has sharp **spines** covering its back.

When you have finished matching the animal stickers to their outlines, place your Task Complete sticker here.

TASK COMPLETE

CLASSIFIED INFORMATION

Scientists who study living things place them into groups. Doing this is called classification. Each group is made up of similar living things. For example, a human and a dog are more alike than a human and a rose. So the human and dog belong to one group (animals) and the rose to another (plants).

PLANT GROUPS

The scientists who study plants are called **botanists**. They divide the plant group into smaller, similar groups—like plants that have flowers or plants that don't make seeds.

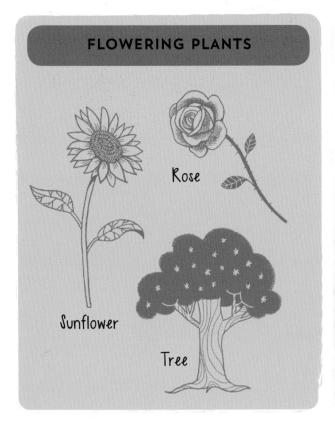

FLOWERING PLANTS

Rose

Sunflower

Tree

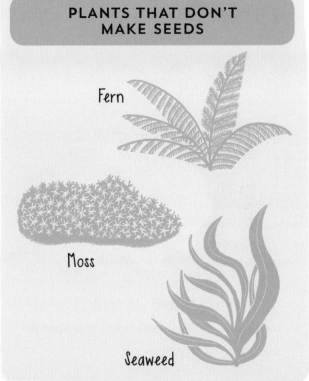

PLANTS THAT DON'T MAKE SEEDS

Fern

Moss

Seaweed

ANIMAL GROUPS

Zoologists (scientists who study animals) divide them into two broad groups: **vertebrates** (animals with a backbone) and **invertebrates** (animals without a backbone). Each group can be split again—for example, vertebrates are either warm-blooded or cold-blooded animals.

WARM-BLOODED ANIMALS

Mammals **Birds**

Cow Ostrich

Tiger Seagull

Whale Eagle

Warm-blooded animals make their own **body heat**. This stays the same temperature, whether the air around them is hot or cold.

COLD-BLOODED ANIMALS

Fish **Reptiles** **Amphibians**

Angelfish Snake Frog

Salmon Turtle Toad

Shark Crocodile Newt

Cold-blooded animals depend on the **temperature** around them for their body heat. They heat up on a warm day and get cooler on a cold day.

-SPORTS-
SCIENCE

The work of sports scientists helps athletes to become fitter, faster and stronger. By understanding how the body works, a sports scientist is able to plan training programs to improve performance and build up strength.

A sports scientist must understand the work the **heart** does and how it performs during exercise. Study this diagram carefully.

The heart is a **pump** that sends blood around the body.

The blood travels through **arteries** (the red lines) carrying oxygen to the muscles.

The blood travels back to the heart through the **veins** (the blue lines).

During exercise, the muscles need more **oxygen,** so the heart needs to beat faster to pump more blood.

RECORDING HEARTBEATS

Now carry out this experiment to see how exercise affects heartbeat. First, you need to make a stethoscope—the instrument a doctor uses to listen to a person's heartbeat.

You need: plastic funnel, paper towel tube, tape, balloon, scissors, timer, a friend.

1. Push the end of the funnel into the tube and tape it in place.

2. Blow up the balloon and then let the air out. This makes it nice and stretchy. Now use the scissors to cut the neck off the balloon.

3. Stretch the balloon over the wide end of the funnel. Make sure it is on tight and then tape it in place.

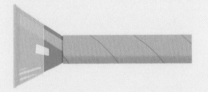

4. Place the wide end of the funnel over your friend's heart and put the end of the tube to your ear. Set the timer and count how many heartbeats there are in 30 seconds. Record the number in the table below.

5. Ask your friend to run on the spot quickly for one minute. When they have finished, use your stethoscope to count how many heartbeats there are in 30 seconds. Record this number.

Now change places and ask your friend to count your heartbeats. Record the results in the table.

When you have made the stethoscope and checked and recorded the heartbeats, place your Task Complete sticker here.

	FRIEND	ME
BEFORE EXERCISE		
AFTER EXERCISE		

TASK COMPLETE

Congratulations! You are now a...

LIFE SCIENTIST
— GRADUATE —

NAME: ------------------------------

The above-named trainee
has now completed the
LIFE SCIENTIST
course.

Scientist Academy would like
to wish you every success
in your career.

GOOD LUCK!

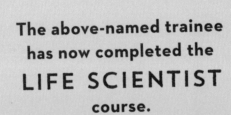

DATE: ------------------------------

WELL DONE!

You have successfully completed all your tasks and finished your trainee scientist's course.

You are now ready to graduate from the Scientist Academy.

AS PART OF YOUR GRADUATION CEREMONY, YOU SHOULD READ THE SCIENTIST'S CODE BELOW AND PROMISE TO FOLLOW IT.

Once you have done this, you can collect your final qualification.

1. When carrying out investigations and experiments, I will work safely and keep myself, other people and all living things free from harm.

2. When collecting evidence and recording data, I will always work with care, patience and accuracy.

3. I will share my discoveries and I will be honest and respectful toward my team and fellow scientists.

4. I understand that new scientific breakthroughs are happening all the time, and I will work hard to keep my knowledge up-to-date and to continue to develop my skills.

5. I will support all scientists in their work and in keeping the Scientist's Code.

Draw or glue a photo of your face here.

SIGNED: _____

SCIENCE FILE

- Press-out Game Cards
- Double-sided Poster
- Sundial Model
  (on the flaps of the book)
- Stickers

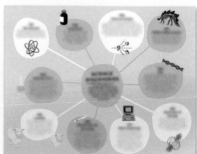

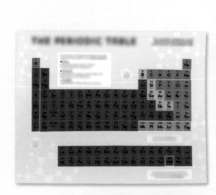

INSTRUCTIONS

SCIENCE PAIRS

1. Shuffle the cards, then place them face-down on a flat surface.
2. Take turns flipping over two cards of your choice. If they are a matching pair, keep them. If not, turn the cards back over. Then the next player can take their turn.
3. The player to collect the most pairs is the winner.

ANSWERS

PLOT THE PATHS P.25

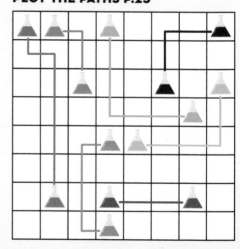